SWAN HUNTER BUILT WARSHIPS

by Ian Buxton

Yard Number 1481, later to be the destroyer ***Express*** living up to her name on full power trials on 2 November 1934 – a valuable £250,000 contract for the builders during the depths of the depression. She became the RCN's ***Gatineau*** in 1943.

Acknowledgements

Ian Rae generously loaned many of the photographs, preserved from his days at the shipyard.
Five photographs are reproduced by permission of Tyne & Wear Archives Service, as acknowledged.

First published in the United Kingdom in 2007 by Maritime Books, Lodge Hill, Liskeard, Cornwall, PL14 4EL

Swan Hunter Built Warships

Although the origins of the shipyards generally known as 'Swans' goes back to 1860, it did not receive its first order from the Admiralty until 1900, a floating dock for Bermuda. In 1874 Charles S. Swan began to build ships at Wallsend on the north bank of the Tyne downstream from Newcastle, encouraged by another shipbuilder, his brother-in-law Charles Mitchell. When Swan fell overboard from a channel ferry and drowned in 1879, George B. Hunter was invited to manage the company, which then became C. S. Swan & Hunter. In the 1890s the company began to build floating docks, so it was that experience that led the Admiralty to place the £225,000 order; the dock was completed in May 1902. By then Hunter had his eye on the order for one of Cunard's new express Atlantic liners, as his company had built up a reputation for high quality passenger-cargo ships. Its near neighbour, Wigham Richardson and Co Ltd had a similar reputation, its Neptune yard having been founded by John Wigham Richardson in 1860. The two companies agreed to merge to give the financial strength and provide the extensive facilities needed to build ***Mauretania***, the largest, fastest and most costly vessel of her day. The new company Swan, Hunter & Wigham Richardson Ltd (SHWR) started in June 1903, also taking over the Tyne Pontoons & Dry Docks repair yard which was sandwiched between the two shipbuilding yards. It also took a majority shareholding in the Wallsend Slipway & Engineering Co Ltd (WSE), just downstream of the Wallsend yard, who were to build ***Mauretania's*** powerful steam turbines.

At the same time, Sir William White was invited to join the SHWR Board, to bring his experience of large fast ships at the Admiralty as the recently retired Director of Naval Construction. At that time, such close connections with the Admiralty or Government precluded a shipyard tendering for warship contracts. Furthermore John Wigham Richardson was a Quaker and thus opposed to building military vessels; his Neptune yard had never built for the Admiralty.

Mauretania was a great technical and commercial success when completed in 1907, so the new company's reputation soared as it moved into the premier league of British shipbuilders. Such a company was well placed to build complex and demanding warships. So following White's resignation from the Board in 1907 and Richardson's death in 1908, SHWR decided to enter the warship building market. With Britain fearful of Germany's naval ambitions and with many warship export orders, it was a good time for warship builders. Hunter lobbied successfully for SHWR's first warship contract, the 755-ton displacement destroyer ***Hope***, ordered in September 1909. Her turbine machinery came from their sister company WSE, constituting over half the total contract value of £92,000 (about £5 million in 2007 money) comparable to a passenger-cargo ship of around 6,000 tons gross. ***Hope*** was delivered in March 1911, and from then until 1920, SHWR was never without a destroyer contract.

After the outbreak of World War 1, the First Lord of the Admiralty, Winston Churchill, and the new First Sea Lord, Admiral 'Jackie' Fisher, instituted a large building programme, requiring the resources of all the major shipbuilders. By the end of 1914, SHWR had received orders for one monitor with 14-inch guns for shore bombardment (***Roberts***), six destroyers and three submarines.

The light cruiser ***Comus*** was the first large warship completed by SHWR, in May 1915. Her Yard Number (YN) was 951, the odd number denoting that she had been built in the Wallsend yard. Although 951 ships had not been built at Wallsend, a new yard number series was started at 708 after the merger by adding together the 296 built at Wallsend and the 411 at Neptune (although the latter included engine contracts in their series). Although all the early SHWR warships were built at Wallsend with machinery mostly from WSE, the demand was such by 1915 that Neptune was brought in to concentrate on sloops, building their steam reciprocating machinery as well as their hulls.

By the end of World War 1, SHWR had completed two cruisers, one monitor, five submarines, 30 destroyers, 16 sloops and five naval auxiliaries. In addition, warship repairs formed a large proportion of the Wallsend drydocks' workload, with 41 cruisers, 74 destroyers and 72 submarines being docked. One major contract was rebuilding the destroyer ***Broke's*** fore end following damage at the Battle of Jutland. All such naval work added significantly to profitability, the three Tyne yards producing around £750,000 annual profits by the end of World War 1, compared with £250,000 prewar, excluding dividends from subsidiaries like WSE and Barclay Curle on the Clyde, acquired in 1912. The labour force had increased to 7500 by October 1915, despite 930 men enlisting in the forces. The last warships ordered from SHWR in World War 1 were either cancelled, including three destroyers, or once launched and engined were towed away to naval dockyards for completion some years later, e.g. ***Whitehall*** at Chatham.

In October 1921, an order was received for one of the four 48,500-ton battlecruisers with nine 16-inch guns, YN 1183. But it was cancelled almost immediately, as the Washington Treaty limiting capital ships was signed shortly afterwards. No further warship contracts were received until 1928 when the destroyer leader ***Codrington*** was ordered, although WSE had completed the machinery for the battleship ***Nelson*** in 1927. The yard kept reasonably busy on merchant ship contracts through the 1920s, financing the construction of many from their wartime profits, such as several Canadian Great Lakes cargo ships. SHWR survived the depression of the early 1930s, partly cushioned by warship orders (including the destroyers ***Esk*** and ***Express*** in 1932), its strong balance sheet, its subsidiary companies and its repair work, which fell off much less than newbuilding during the shipping slump. Pioneering work in welded ship construction was undertaken in the 1930s.

The next large warship order was for the 6830-ton cruiser ***Phaeton*** in 1933, thereafter to be transferred to the Royal Australian Navy as ***Sydney***. After her completion in 1935, re-armament produced a steady flow of subsequent warship orders, including the battleship ***Jellicoe*** (later renamed ***Anson***) and the cruisers ***Edinburgh*** and ***Mauritius***. World War 2 saw SHWR as one of the big five warship builders (the others were Vickers-Armstrongs, Harland & Wolff, Cammell Laird and John Brown). The Wallsend yard concentrated largely on front line ships like cruisers and destroyers, while Neptune built frigates and auxiliary vessels like cable ships, as well as merchant vessels. A vessel type new to SHWR was the aircraft carrier, including the light fleet carrier ***Vengeance*** completed in 1944 and escort carrier ***Vindex***. The labour force at the two shipbuilding yards in 1943 averaged 5,500 men, 80% on warship work.

The repair yard was equally busy, by then with three graving and one floating dock. No. 2 graving dock was reserved largely for submarines, destroyers and minesweepers. As well as pre-delivery dockings of new ships for many of the Tyne shipyards, major repairs included the destroyer ***Achates*** whose fore end had been blown off by a mine (repaired 9.41 - 4.42) and destroyer ***Marne*** whose aft end was rebuilt after torpedo damage (3.43 - 1.44). Ships completed during World War 2 amounted to 81 naval vessels - one battleship, two carriers, three cruisers (a fourth, ***Superb***, completing in November 1945), 28 destroyers, six escorts, 27 landing vessels and 14 auxiliaries, plus 43 merchant ships.

As in 1919, many naval contracts were cancelled at the end of World War 2, to allow shipyards to concentrate on merchant ship work - swords into ploughshares. Lead ship of her class, the destroyer ***Daring*** had been ordered in January 1945, but she was not launched until 1949 and completed in 1952. Construction of the carrier ***Albion*** was suspended after launch in May 1947, so she was not completed until 1954, although by then able to operate jet aircraft.

The first postwar warship order was in 1951 for two Type 14 anti-submarine frigates ***Pellew*** and ***Russell***, engined by WSE. Scotts at Greenock had launched the cruiser ***Defence*** in 1944, but construction was suspended awaiting the development of new rapid firing 6-inch and 3-inch guns. In 1954 the contract for her completion was awarded to SHWR as YN 1859. She was completed as ***Lion*** in 1960, one of a class of three, the last gun armed cruisers for the RN. The 1960s saw further warship orders, including the surface-air missile armed destroyers ***London***, ***Norfolk*** and ***Bristol***, the latter bearing the last yard number of the original SHWR series, 2030.

Concerned about the competitiveness of the British shipbuilding industry, the Government had commissioned the Geddes Report, published in 1966. This recommended larger shipyard groupings, so SHWR chairman Sir John Hunter (George Hunter's grandson) set about creating a major international shipbuilding and shiprepair group. SHWR was the natural leader of a Tyne-based group, having already acquired Smiths Dock with yards on the Tees and the Tyne in 1966, and in 1967 small shipbuilder Cleland's, just downstream of WSE, and Readhead's, at South Shields. It had dropped the SHWR title in 1966 in favour of the short-lived titles of Associated Shipbuilders, and Swan Hunter (Shipbuilders) Ltd. Then on 1 January 1968, Swan Hunter & Tyne Shipbuilders Ltd came into existence, incorporating the former Vickers Walker and Hawthorn Leslie Hebburn yards, as well as Wallsend, Neptune and South Shields yards. A new series of yard numbers was started at 1 in 1967. The title was simplified to Swan Hunter Shipbuilders Ltd in 1969 (SHS) after the Furness yard on the Tees was taken over.

The first Ministry of Defence (MoD) orders for the new group was an £8M contract for three 7,500 ton oilers, YNs 5, 6 and 7, named ***Green***, ***Grey*** and ***Blue Rovers***. The first warships were the two Type 42 Sea Dart destroyers ***Newcastle*** and ***Glasgow***, ordered in 1971. By then the international shipbuilding market was booming, especially with orders for tankers. Swans undertook a major yard modernisation process in the early 1970s to meet the demand, which included 250,000-tonne deadweight tankers, although these slowed progress on the naval orders. But, in 1974, everything changed following the fourfold rise in oil prices. Shipping markets slumped, tanker orders were cancelled, shipbuilding prices fell as builders scrambled for the few new orders around, while supply increased with new entrants to the market like Korea determined to buy orders at any price. The result was that naval shipbuilding was one of the few profitable sectors for British shipyards. Although the MoD did not award 'cost plus' contracts to SHWR, the escalation clauses in their contracts did at least protect the shipbuilder from rapid inflation of material and labour costs, unlike fixed price merchant ship orders. Design changes during construction brought additional revenue for 'extras'. Although Swans fought against the nationalisation of the British shipbuilding industry in 1977, to most builders it came as a welcome relief from increasing losses.

Swan Hunter Shipbuilders had already received an order in 1976 for the second 'through deck cruiser' or anti-submarine carrier ***Illustrious***, capable of carrying Sea King helicopters and the new short take-off and vertical landing Sea Harrier. A third vessel ***Ark Royal*** was ordered in 1978 after nationalisation, making her the highest value contract ever placed with Swans at over £200 million (which excluded MoD furnished equipment like weapon systems, main engines and gearing). Both were completed under the nationalised British Shipbuilders (BS) banner, the former (***Illustrious***) rushed to completion in June 1982 to relieve ***Invincible*** off the Falklands, the latter (***Ark Royal***) in July 1985. Post Falklands replacement orders at SHS included the frigates ***Sheffield*** and ***Coventry*** (although as Type 22 anti-submarine frigates rather than the Type 42 destroyers of their namesakes), logistic vessel ***Sir Galahad*** and the container-roro ***Atlantic Conveyor***.

SHS had been an early user of computer aided design systems, especially for large tanker design. Faced with low international prices for merchant ships and internal BS competition for warship orders, SHS sought means to integrate design with production, to increase productivity (output per man) which would not only lower costs when tendering, but speed up delivery. One of the main routes was pre-outfitting of large hull units or modules, so that pipework, auxiliary machinery and fittings were installed in blocks of steel structure under cover in the workshops, and then rolled out to the berth on multi-wheel trailers, to be lifted into place by 180-tonne cranes. The traditional method of outfitting an empty steel shell after launch was much slower and more labour intensive, while quality was more difficult to control. Although requiring much more effort in work preparation, material ordering and planning, significant cost and time savings were obtained by pre-outfitting modules.

By 1986 British Shipbuilders had closed many of its merchant shipbuilding yards in the face of mounting losses, and was privatising the warship builders. The former Hawthorn Leslie, Vickers (Walker) and Readhead yards had all been closed by 1985, leaving just the original Wallsend and Neptune yards. Some of SHS managers under Dr Roger Vaughan considered the prospects good; merchant ship orders and prices had recovered somewhat, while the MoD had started ordering Type 23 frigates as well as auxiliaries. Retaining the same title under privatisation, Swan Hunter Shipbuilders Ltd obtained orders for a cable ship, a research vessel and their first Type 23 frigate ***Marlborough***, maintaining employment for about 4,000 men.

SHS had expected to become the lead yard for the two Auxiliary Oiler Replenishment vessels (AOR) with a good design and a competitive price. But politics intervened and the order for ***Fort Victoria*** was placed with Harland & Wolff at Belfast in 1986, with a contract price and delivery date that were unrealistic, given that yard's lack of recent experience of MoD newbuilding work. SHS had to make do (20 months later) with the order for the second ship ***Fort George*** at a price that reflected H&W's low bid. In the event ***Fort Victoria*** was late and well over budget, only being delivered a few days before ***Fort George*** in March 1993.

Three more Type 23s were ordered in December 1989, by which time productivity gains were showing through in prices relatively lower than early ships, with deliveries due in 1993-4. The company put much effort into pursuing overseas naval orders for patrol vessels and auxiliaries, but without success. The next major MoD order was for the Landing Platform Helicopter ship ***Ocean***. SHS reckoned they could beat Vickers Shipbuilding & Engineering Ltd (VSEL) at Barrow with a better design, lower building costs and earlier delivery. But cash flow was tight following problems with the Antarctic research vessels ***James Clark Ross*** and renegotiation of the ***Fort George*** contract, while the overdraft was mounting at the bank. SHS' price had to reflect not only material and labour costs, but a large overhead cost and a reasonable profit margin. But VSEL having only built submarines since 1982 was determined to get back into building surface ships, especially as work on the Trident submarines was tailing off. With deeper pockets than Swan's, they put in a loss making bid well below cost to 'buy' the work. After a second round of best and final bids in April 1993, SHS put in a realistic £210 million while VSEL put in £144 million. There was no option for the MoD but to choose the VSEL bid, despite cries of 'foul' from Tyneside. VSEL subcontracted the hull to Kvaerner Govan on the Clyde; it is probable that the final cost to the company was over £200 million, thus incurring substantial losses.

But it was too late for SHS, their lifeline had gone, the banks would not increase the existing £11 million overdraft, so receivers Price Waterhouse were called in by SHS creditors in May 1993. Although there were some immediate redundancies, many of the 1000-plus employees were kept on by the receiver to complete the frigates ***Westminster***, ***Northumberland*** and ***Richmond***, all of which had been launched. When the latter sailed from Wallsend on 3 November 1994, it looked like the end of shipbuilding on the Tyne. As the receivers were obliged to recover as much money as possible for SHS' creditors, they hoped to sell the yard as a going concern. Although there were some nibbles, no serious bidders had appeared by early 1995, so it was arranged to auction the shipyard and all its equipment in June. Shortly before the auction, Dutchman Jaap Kroese, who had successfully operated the THC offshore yard at Hartlepool, put in a £5 million bid for the Wallsend site, which was accepted.

The new company called Swan Hunter (Tyneside) Ltd initially worked on conversions such as the pipelayer ***Solitaire*** and on the dismantling of oil rigs. Then the opportunity came to get back into shipbuilding by tendering for two new Auxiliary Landing Ships (Logistic) - mini versions of Landing Platform Dock ships, capable of taking landing craft in a floodable dock. Without the design staff of the old SHS and no experience of naval vessel construction, a design was bought from the De Schelde shipyard in Holland. An overly optimistic price and delivery date was quoted for two vessels, ***Largs Bay*** and ***Lyme Bay***. The MoD placed an order for the two ships in December 2000 for a reported price of £160 million for the two with delivery of the first due in January 2004. Later two follow-on vessels were ordered from BAE Systems on the Clyde.

The company decided to adopt a new ship construction philosophy, whereby modules were erected in a floating dock which was then moved into the river and flooded down to allow the hull to be floated off. The main building slipway which had been used for big tankers and the carriers was dug up to create a basin for the floating dock, which had been bought secondhand from Dunkirk. 12-metre long 'ring' units (i.e. a complete cross-section of the main hull) were rolled in succession into the dock. ***Largs Bay*** (YN 141) was floated out of its dock on 18 July 2003 amidst great local publicity. The vessel was little more than a steel shell however with minimal pre-outfit, typical of shipbuilding in the 1960s, so a large amount of labour-intensive outfitting remained to be completed, leading to cost overruns. At the end of 2004, the Ministry of Defence were forced to pay an extra £84 million to Swans to complete the ships.

Even this was not enough to complete both ships, although ***Largs Bay*** was handed over in April 2006, two years late. By then the Ministry of Defence had lost patience with Swans, especially as BAE had already completed the 'follow on' ship ***Mounts Bay*** in December 2005. The cost of the two ships had roughly doubled from the original price, so the contract for ***Lyme Bay*** was cancelled. The uncompleted hull was towed out of the Tyne on 17 July 2006 to be completed by BAE on the Clyde. This event almost certainly marked the end of new ship building on the Tyne, after 146 years of the former Swan Hunter and Wigham Richardson companies. The 'new' Swan Hunter had no connection with the previous companies other than using the site and the name. Its experience was in the offshore industry, with neither experience of shipbuilding nor of MoD work. While the new company provided some employment and training, it was at great expense to the taxpayer, while delivery of the ships to the RFA was much delayed. The company announced in late 2006 that it was selling its cranes and much of its shipbuilding plant.

Altogether a sad end to a proud heritage of shipbuilding on the River Tyne.

Ian Buxton
October 2007

Naval Vessels built by Swan Hunter

Type	**1900 - 1949**	**1950 - 2006**
Battleship, aircraft carriers, cruisers, monitor	13½	3½
Destroyers	77	8½
Frigates and Escorts	27	11
Submarines	5	
Landing ships and craft	30	2½
Fleet auxiliaries and oilers	7	11
Misc Admiralty vessels including dockyard caissons	14½	
Floating docks	7	
Total	**181**	**36½**

Vessels launched elsewhere but completed by Swans, or launched by Swans but not completed by them or cancelled incomplete, counted as ½. Excludes Vickers and Hawthorn Leslie pre merger.

Swan Hunter's very first Admiralty contract, the Bermuda floating dock, was ordered in December 1900 as Yard Number 262 to a Clark & Standfield design. It had a clear breadth of 93ft and was designed to lift a vessel displacing up to 17500 tons, which covered all the pre-dreadnoughts of the day. The dock is seen being tested in the Medway by lifting ***Sans Pareil*** on 5 July 1902. It arrived at Bermuda on 8 August 1902 to replace the 1869-built floating dock, although it did not enter service until 1906. It was numbered ***AFD 1*** in 1925, remaining in service until 1946 when it was replaced by ***AFD 5***.

Berths 5 and 6 to the east of the large gantry were often used to build destroyers. K class ***Shark*** (YN 903), ***Sparrowhawk*** (905) and ***Spitfire*** (907) have their plating nearly finished in this photograph taken in mid 1912. Note the lack of any heavy lifting appliances; their structural scantlings were light, while heavy weights such as machinery were shipped after launch under big cranes.

L class ***Sandfly*** (YN 875) was Swan Hunter & Wigham Richardson Ltd's (SHWR) second destroyer completed in December 1911 at a modest 750 tons displacement; a sister of their first warship, ***Hope***. Unlike some of the other warship builders with longer experience of the Admiralty's needs, SHWR were content to build to Admiralty destroyer designs.

The Fourth Destroyer Flotilla in the Solent in April 1914, with three SHWR destroyers, ***Shark*** leading, ***Sparrowhawk*** third and ***Spitfire*** fifth. The first two were lost at Jutland in 1916, with ***Spitfire*** being broken up in 1921 under a large postwar clearout of obsolescent ships.

After taking over Tyne Pontoons in 1903, SHWR built up its shiprepairing division. A second graving dock 490ft long was added to the existing 1887 drydock, and two floating docks. Here the light cruiser ***Nottingham*** had recently been completed at Pembroke Dock, but engined by the Tyne's Hawthorn Leslie. She was the first ship to enter the new No.2 dock on 17 September 1914. The drydocks were extensively used for warship repairs during WW1. ***Nottingham*** herself was torpedoed in 1916.

The C class cruiser ***Comus*** (YN 951) virtually complete on 5 May 1915, SHWR's first cruiser. She had been launched on 12 December 1914 off the large covered No.2 berth seen on the left. Her steam turbine machinery (which was to give her 28.5 knots) was built by SHWR's subsidiary Wallsend Slipway & Engineering Co Ltd (WSE). She was with the Grand Fleet during WW1, remaining in service for most of the 1920s before being scrapped at Barrow in 1934.

Early in WW1, Churchill (First Lord of the Admiralty) and Fisher (First Sea Lord) were keen to build a fleet of big gun monitors for the coastal bombardment of enemy held territory. SHWR offered to build one of four 6,150-ton monitors armed with one twin 14-inch turret purchased from Bethlehem Steel in the US. Yard Number 991 ***Stonewall Jackson*** was launched only four months after keel laying. Here she gets her final touches alongside the Wallsend yard in June 1915, before departing for the Dardanelles under her new name of ***Roberts***. As essentially a 'hostilities-only' type, most of the big monitors were paid off at the end of WW1, although ***Roberts*** lingered in experimental roles until scrapped in 1936.

SHWR's Neptune yard built ten sloops up to 1919, despite its founder the late John Wigham Richardson being a Quaker who would not build warships before the 1903 merger. ***Flying Fox*** (YN 1056), also engined by Neptune, was completed in May 1918. The vessels were designed with a generally symmetric profile fore and aft, intended with dazzle painting to make it difficult for the enemy to estimate course and speed. Few remained in the postwar navy; many were sold for commercial service or scrapped at less than ten years old. ***Flying Fox*** was used as a RNVR drillship at Bristol until scrapped in 1973.

The destroyer ***Tower*** (YN 1027) uses the full 27,000 shp of her Brown-Curtis turbines from WSE (Engine No. 774) on trial on 11 August 1917. Her twin screw machinery had been shipped on board at their works just downstream of SHWR between 10 April (a week after launch) and 8 May 1917. None of the eleven modified R class survived more than a dozen years, ***Tower*** being scrapped at Newport in 1928.

The destroyer ***Tilbury*** (YN 1081) makes an impressive sight on full power trials off the Tyne on 17 September 1918. The boat of Frank & Son of South Shields, the photographer, is about to get the full force of the wash. Despite her T name, she was actually of the Admiralty S class of 1075 tons, armed with three 4-inch guns and four torpedo tubes. She saw only a few weeks' service before the end of the war and was scrapped in 1931.

Vimiera, SHWR's first V&W class destroyer (YN 1043), makes a stirring sight with smoke from her three oil-fired (not coal-fired!) boilers on trials on 13 September 1917. Her machinery was built by Parsons Marine Steam Turbine Co, whose works were just downstream of the Wallsend yard. The V&W destroyers incorporated WW1 experience to date. Many of the earlier destroyers were found to be wet ships at sea, so freeboard and forecastle height was increased in the V&W class. Ships of this well balanced design remained in service until the end of WW2.

The destroyer ***Sparrowhawk*** (YN 1071) on trials off the Tyne on 4 September 1918. Her 27,000-shp steam turbine machinery came from WSE, costing £98,000, more than the £92,000 of her hull. At that time, the purchasing power of the pound was about 60 times higher than today.

Another of the 55 Admiralty S class destroyers, ***Splendid*** (YN 1073) runs her trials on 29 October 1918. With too many obsolescent destroyers left over after WW1, she lasted barely a dozen years before being scrapped at Charlestown on the Forth in 1931. Metal Industries paid only £3,500 for her, 2% of her building cost, reflecting the depression of scrap prices during the slump.

The Admiralty S class destroyer ***Sportive*** (YN 1085) must be making over 30 knots in this trials photograph of 17 December 1918. Too late for service in WW1, she was scrapped in 1936, being handed over with 23 other destroyers to breakers T W Ward in part payment for the ex Cunard White Star liner ***Majestic*** recently purchased by Ward, which the Admiralty wished to convert to a training ship (***Caledonia***).

SHWR built two C class cruisers in WW1, ***Comus*** and ***Coventry***. YN 1035 ***Coventry*** had a more efficient propulsion system with 40,000-shp twin screw geared Brown-Curtis steam turbines in place of ***Comus***' quadruple screw direct drive turbines. Both sets were built by WSE. She is seen here on trials in February 1918. The Admiralty paid SHWR £500,000 for the ship (i.e. excluding armament and naval fittings), 44% of which went to WSE for the machinery. She was briefly with the 5th Light Cruiser Squadron at Harwich, then spent most of the 1920s in the Mediterranean. She was converted into an anti-aircraft cruiser in 1936, her 6-inch low angle guns giving way to the 4-inch high angle weapon. She was bombed and sunk by Italian aircraft off Tobruk on 14 September 1942.

The L class submarine ***L.5*** (YN 1037) was the fourth submarine built by SHWR, viewed inside the Tyne breakwaters in May 1918. Her twin 12-cylinder 2400 bhp diesels were built by Crossley of Manchester, although those for her sister ***L.33*** were built by SHWR's Neptune engine works. The L class incorporated experience from the large number of E class submarines, but with new submarine classes beginning to come forward in the 1930s, most of the L class were scrapped. ***L.5*** and her Vicker's built sister ***L.3*** were sold to Metal Industries on 29 August 1930 for breaking up on the Forth.

The destroyer ***Shark*** (YN 1069) with steam up on 11 July 1918 about to depart from Wallsend yard, having commissioned on 29 June. She perpetuated the name of the 1913 SHWR destroyer ***Shark***. Inboard is probably ***Sparrowhawk***. The two covered berths (No. 8 and 9) date from the 1890s.

A busy scene alongside the Wallsend yard in June 1919. Nearest is submarine ***L.33*** (YN 1067) launched on 21 May. Beyond lie ***Whitshed*** (outboard, YN 1103) and another V&W, possibly ***Wild Swan***. The covered berths behind were erected in 1904 to build ***Mauretania***.

The Modified W class destroyer ***Whitshed*** (YN 1103) on trials on 11 July 1919 after the end of WW1. Her cost to the Admiralty was £112,000 (from SHWR) for the hull, and £105,500 (from WSE) for machinery. This group of ships mounted four 4.7-inch instead of 4-inch guns. The design was well balanced, many remaining in service for 25 years. She survived WW2, being scrapped on the Tyne in 1948.

Another modified W class on trials, ***Wild Swan*** (YN 1105) on 14 November 1919. Like many of SHWR's WW1 destroyers, she was engined by their subsidiary Wallsend Slipway, with 27,000 shp Brown-Curtis turbines. A revised layout of boilers with two in the forward boiler room and one in the after, resulted in a more pleasing funnel profile, compared with the V class like ***Vimiera*** with one thin forward funnel, serving a single boiler in the forward room.

SHWR had built up a reputation for building floating docks. Six were built new for the Admiralty, and another taken over in 1916 for service at Invergordon. YN 1321 ***AFD IX*** was the largest, a 50,000-ton lift dock for the new base at Singapore, capable of lifting the largest battleship or aircraft carrier. Launched in seven sections during 1927, it is seen here in June 1928, berthed downriver of the cross-river ferry landing, ready for its 4-month tow in two parts to Singapore. The dock was scuttled on 29th January 1942, but raised by the Japanese invaders, then sunk by US aircraft in 1945. It was salvaged in 1952-54 and scrapped. Two more AFDs (***23*** and ***35***) were built to this design in WW2 in India.

A beautifully clear broadside view of the sloop ***Scarborough*** (YN 1407) leaving the Tyne on 31 July 1930, taken by photographers Frank & Sons of South Shields. She and her sister ***Folkestone*** (completed the previous month) were designed for both escort and minesweeping duties. She was used for surveying in 1939, but took up anti-submarine operations during WW2. She was scrapped at Stockton in 1949.

The light cruiser ***Sydney*** (YN 1487) heads out of the Tyne in the summer of 1935, possibly for trials as her paint scheme looks incomplete. Laid down as ***Phaeton*** for the RN, she was completed for the Royal Australian Navy. She was sunk by the German raider ***Kormoran*** off western Australia in 1941. Controversy continues to this day as to how she came to be lost with all her crew. Her sisters ***Perth*** and ***Hobart*** were built at Portsmouth and Devonport Dockyards respectively.

Destroyers were usually ordered in pairs between the wars. YN 1505 ***Hyperion*** takes to the water on 8 April 1936, six weeks after her sister ***Hunter***. Both a paddle tug and a screw tug are in attendance to manoeuvre her alongside the fitting out wharf. From her light draft, it can be seen that her machinery has yet to be shipped. She took part in the Spanish Civil War patrols 1937-39, before being lost in the Mediterranean in 1940. The vessel in the background is the passenger-cargo ship ***Matua***, nearly completed at the Hawthorn Leslie shipyard.

SHWR built only two of the 20 British built Tribal class destroyers. Here a gleaming newly completed ***Tartar*** (YN 1529) passes North Shields in March 1939, soon to go to war. Like all SHWR's destroyers post-WW1, she was engined by their subsidiary Wallsend Slipway & Engineering, as their No. 923. ***Tartar*** was one of only three RN Tribals to survive the war, being scrapped at Newport in 1948.

The Tribal class destroyer ***Somali*** (YN 1527) at the end of 1938, still in her builder's hands, as indicated by the Red Ensign on the mainmast. She was well used as a fleet escort, before being torpedoed in the Greenland Sea on 20 September 1942 while escorting Arctic convoy QP 14.

SHWR built two J/K class destroyers - ***Janus*** and ***Khartoum***. The former (YN 1549) is seen on 9 November 1938, one day before launching. Her propeller shafts and rudder have been fitted, but the propellers will await fitting in drydock after her machinery has been installed. She was completed on 4 Aug 1939 shortly before the outbreak of war.

Khartoum (YN 1551) just launched from Wallsend yard on 6 February 1939. This is believed to be one of the few (only?) pictures of the destroyer which was completed in November 1939. Wartime censorship restricted photography; she was lost in June 1940 soon after completion. Behind her bow can be seen the hull of the cruiser ***Naiad*** launched three days earlier at Hawthorn Leslie.

The destroyer ***Janus*** (YN 1549) at full speed on 5 August 1939. She made 34.1 knots with 40411 shp from her Wallsend Slipway turbines. By mid 1940 the J class was heavily engaged in the Mediterranean. She was lost to a Hs293 glider bomb off Anzio on 23 January 1944.

The cruiser ***Edinburgh*** (YN 1537) looking somewhat bare with minimal rig and no directors - construction of the latter probably delayed at Vickers-Armstrongs. She looks as if she is leaving for preliminary trials in March 1939. After acceptance in July, she returned to the Tyne for repairs to her structure and armour plating at Middle Docks from March-October 1940. She was torpedoed and sunk in the Barents Sea in May 1942. Her only sister ***Belfast*** survives as a museum ship on the Thames.

SHWR completed three Colony class 8,000-ton cruisers during WW2. YN 1565 ***Mauritius*** was the first to be launched on 19 July 1939. Her side armour has already been fitted, but no machinery or armament, so she is seen floating at a draft of only about 10 feet, half of that when fully loaded. She was not completed until January 1941, Churchill having ordered the suspension of construction of larger warships in 1940 to allow smaller vessels to be completed more quickly.

The destroyer ***Jervis*** had been completed at Hawthorn Leslie in 1939. She was in collision with a tanker on 23 March 1940 off Norway and had to spend three months under repair in SHWR's No.1 drydock, until 23 June. Only two of the eight J class survived the war, she being scrapped on the Clyde in 1949 after target trials. The drydock opened in 1887, finally closing in 2004, latterly under A&P Tyne ownership.

The early tank landing craft were built by regular shipbuilders like SHWR, although the majority were later constructed by structural steel firms on the Tees and Clyde, to free up resources for more complex vessels. SHWR built four LCT Mark 2 in 1941, originally designated ***TLC 35-38***. Here YN 1657 ***TLC 38***, by then renamed ***LCT 107***, heads downriver on 6 August 1941. She was lost with her sister ***LCT 106*** off Benghazi in 1943. The 296-ton vessels could carry seven tanks. Although most of the LCTs had twin screw diesel propulsion, the SHWR vessels had triple screw petrol engines, always a dangerous fuel for ships, although giving them an extra knot of speed.

SHWR built sixteen Hunt class escort destroyers during WW2 before concentrating on Fleet destroyers. ***Lamerton*** (YN 1587) was a Type 2, mounting the full designed six 4-inch guns, having been widened from the 29ft of the Type 1s to 31ft 6in to correct stability deficiencies. She poses here in the Tyne on 13 August 1941, sporting the non-rotating Type 286 surface warning radar aerial at her masthead. Although with lesser armament, speed and endurance than the Fleet destroyers, they could be built more quickly.

One of the three Type 3 Hunts built by SHWR which were handed over to the Greek Navy, although ordered for the RN on 28 Jul 1940. ***Miaoulis*** (ex ***Modbury*** YN 1649) was the last SHWR Hunt to be completed. Seen here in the Tyne on 16 November 1942, her two twin 4-inch guns trained on the beam as required by the censor for photographs at that time. She was notionally returned to the RN before being scrapped in Greece in 1961.

SHWR's only Type 3 Hunt completed for the RN was YN 1647 ***Melbreak***, posing for her photo on 7 October 1942. By this time shipyards were being permitted to photograph completed ships, although referring to her only by her J Number 4293, the security identification used for naval vessels under construction in WW2. She seems to have a full outfit of depth charges, and left the river three days later. She spent most of the war based at Plymouth. She saw no post-war operational service before being scrapped in 1956.

Professional photographer J H Cleet from South Shields took this photo of ***Queenborough*** (YN 1605) on 6 December 1942. After printing the required number of photos, Cleet had to hand over his negatives for destruction, which partly explains the rth of wartime photographs of the Tyne. She was transferred to the Royal Australian Navy in 1945, and converted to a fast anti-submarine Type 15 frigate by Cockatoo Dockyard in Sydney in 1954.

Most WW2 Fleet destroyers were ordered in pairs from experienced warship builders like SHWR, who received the order for ***Quality*** (YN 1603) on 2 April 1940. She poses off Jarrow Slake on 30 August 1942, 4.7-inch guns and quadruple pom-pom A/A weapons trained to starboard. She joined the Royal Australian Navy in 1945, but was not converted to a fast frigate, being scrapped in Japan in 1958.

SHWR built only one battleship, one of the King George V class originally to have been named ***Jellicoe*** (YN 1553) when ordered on 28 April 1937. Unfortunately no construction photos have been found. As they had no large fitting out crane, the 150-ton floating crane ***Titan*** was used to lift machinery components, armour plates and 5.25-inch gun mountings onboard. The four twin 5.25-inch mountings built by Vickers-Armstrongs at Elswick upriver were so lifted, as were the four built by Harland & Wolff in Glasgow and shipped to the Tyne in coasters. However, most of the heavier 14-inch mounting components were lifted by Vickers-Armstrong's 250-ton crane at the Naval Yard, Walker. Renamed ***Anson***, she left the Tyne on 3 May 1942 for drydocking at Rosyth and brief trials before entering service on 22 June.

No building photos of YN 1575 ***Gambia*** have been found. She was laid down on 24 July 1939, just five days after ***Mauritius*** had been launched from the same No.3 Berth, leaving the Tyne on 17 February 1942. She served in the Royal New Zealand Navy from 1943-46. In this 1957 view taken in the Clyde, she has lost her X turret and aircraft, while her bridge has been remodelled and close range guns updated from pom-poms to Bofors. She was scrapped at Inverkeithing in 1968.

A murky but rare view of cruiser ***Newfoundland*** (YN 1589) leaving the Tyne on 15 January 1943, completed with only three triple 6-inch turrets built by Vickers-Armstrongs at Elswick, and without aircraft. She served in various flagship roles around the world until paying off in 1959. She was then sold to become the Peruvian ***Almirante Grau***.

Eight aircraft carriers were ordered from SHWR during WW2, four light fleet carriers (one cancelled, ***Arrogant***), two MAC ships, one escort carrier and one conversion. The latter was ***Pretoria Castle*** completed by Harland & Wolff at Belfast as a 17,392-grt passenger liner for Union Castle in March 1939 and then converted into an armed merchant cruiser in October 1939. SHWR converted her to an escort carrier at Wallsend from July 1942. Here she lies alongside Neptune yard in mid 1943, with two of the gantries covering the shipbuilding berths visible.

Pretoria Castle leaves the yard on 12 August 1943, fully armed and capable of carrying 21 aircraft. She was used mainly as a training and trials carrier. She was converted back into a passenger-cargo liner in 1947 by Harland and Wolff, Belfast, and renamed ***Warwick Castle.***

MAC ships or merchant aircraft carriers were merchant ships onto which was built a flight deck and basic aviation facilities for operating four Swordfish aircraft. Four had been built as tankers, so were still able to operate as cargo carriers. Here YN 1726 ***Empire MacCabe*** was built at the Neptune yard, indicated by the even yard number. ***Empire MacCabe*** was completed in November 1943, managed by the British Tanker Co (now BP), becoming their tanker ***British Escort*** in 1946. Her cost to the Ministry of War Transport was £438,000, or about £50,000 more than a conventional tanker.

Empire MacCabe's near sister, the 8,856 gross ton ***Empire MacMahon***, was built at the Wallsend yard with the odd numbered YN 1677. Tugs take her down-river at light draft on a sunny day in December 1943. She was managed by Anglo-Saxon Petroleum (now Shell), becoming their tanker ***Naninia*** in 1946. She served them until 1960 before being superseded by much larger tankers.

The T class destroyer ***Tuscan*** (YN 1663) on 5 March 1943, six days before she left the Tyne. The eight T class, including her SHWR sister ***Tyrian***, formed the 24th Destryoer Flotilla of the British Pacific Fleet in 1945. She was partially converted to a fast anti-submarine frigate in 1953 at Cardiff and scrapped in 1966 at Boness on the Forth.

The U class destroyer ***Grenville*** (YN 1669) poses in the Tyne on 21 May 1943, with a tripod mast forward but lattice aft for her high frequency direction finding aerial. She is already loaded with depth charges and mounts the Dutch designed Hazemeyer twin 40mm gun between her torpedo tubes. This class also saw service with the British Pacific Fleet in 1945. She was fully converted into a Type 15 frigate at Devonport in 1954. From 1969 she was used for anti-submarine trials, until scrapped at Rochester in 1983.

The V class destroyer ***Vigilant*** (YN 1679) in the Tyne on 4 September 1943, now with lattice mast forward for her Types 272 and 291 (at masthead) radar. She served in the East Indies Fleet in 1945. Like so many Fleet destroyers, she was converted into a fast A/S frigate, in 1952 at Southampton. She was scrapped at Faslane in 1965, along with her Swan Hunter sister, ***Virago***.

Three Castle class corvettes were ordered from SHWR, so that their greater warship experience and drawing office resources would assist the less experienced builders who built most of the class. Here ***Portchester Castle*** (YN 1778) displays her hull form with production-friendly straight line sheer, after her launch from Neptune yard on 21 June 1943. SHWR Neptune engine works built her 4-cylinder 2750 ihp triple expansion engine, of a standard design used in most corvettes and frigates. Longer and more seaworthy than a Flower class corvette, she was used in training roles into the 1950s, before scrapping at Troon in 1958. The first Castle to be completed, ***Hadleigh Castle***, was launched by Smith's Dock on the Tees on the same day.

SHWR's second Castle, ***Rushen Castle*** (YN 1780) departs on 17 February 1944, bringing to the Battle of the Atlantic her new Squid ahead throwing mortar – just visible under its black cover on the deck above her 4-inch gun. She was converted to the ocean weather ship ***Weather Surveyor*** at Blyth in 1961.

Although most Loch class vessels were built by "second division" shipbuilders, eight of these 1435-ton twin screw frigates were ordered from SHWR's Neptune yard on 13 February 1943. Three were subsequently cancelled and two completed as coastal forces depot ships. YN 1786 ***Loch Shin***, seen here on 5 Oct 1944 about to leave the Tyne, is in her original anti-submarine form. She became New Zealand's ***Taupo*** in 1948, before being scrapped in Japan in 1961.

SHWR's third Loch class was YN 1788 ***Loch Cree***, completed as the South African Navy's ***Natal***, seen here about to depart the Tyne on 14 March 1945. On her way to Rosyth later that day, she sank ***U-714*** with her Squid anti-submarine mortars. Although the U-boat had been located and prepared for the kill by the escort destroyer ***Wivern***, ***Natal*** was allowed to take all the credit for propaganda purposes. She was converted to a survey vessel in 1957. She was sunk as a target off Simons Town in 1972 after her replacement ***Protea*** was completed.

The fourth and fifth SHWR Lochs were completed as depot ships for coastal forces, with the decline in the need for more anti-submarine escorts, YN 1790 ***Derby Haven*** having been ordered as ***Loch Assynt***. She is seen here just after launch from Neptune yard on 14 December 1944, with ***LST 3020*** astern being temporarily moved from the fitting out quay for the launch. She became the Iranian ***Babr*** in 1949.

Loch Torridon (YN 1792) was also completed as a 1652-ton depot ship, ***Woodbridge Haven***, with larger superstructure for workshops and offices, but reduced armament. Seen here on 16 October 1945, she sports the blue Pacific camouflage panel. She left on 24 October for active service. She became a submarine target ship in the Clyde in the 1950s. By 1955 she had commissioned as the Headquraters ship of the 2nd Minesweeping Squadron. Following similar service in the Mediterranean (1957-60) and the Far Eat (1960-63) she was eventally towed from Portsmouth to Blyth in 1965 to be broken up.

SHWR was the lead yard for the Landing Ship Tank Mark 3. They were initially known as Transport Ferries to avoid shipyard workers claiming the higher wages accorded to tank landing craft builders at steel fabricators. Two corvette/frigate 2,750ihp steam reciprocating engines built by the Neptune engine works were fitted, which were more readily available than the diesels used in the US-built LST.2s. ***TF 19*** (YN 1818) is photographed here as ***LST 3019*** on 22 December 1944. Most LSTs were given names after WW2, ***LST 3019*** being named ***Vaagso*** (after the Commando raid) in 1947.

Vengeance (YN 1699) was SHWR's first aircraft carrier designed as such. The second of her class to be completed, she lies here in the Tyne on 22 December 1944, before leaving the river on 4 January 1945. She formed part of the 11th Aircraft Carrier Squadron of the British Pacific Fleet. She survived another 60 years, becoming the Brazilian ***Minas Gerais*** in 1957, before being scrapped on Alang beach in India in 2004.

Light fleet carrier ***Leviathan*** (YN 1703) slides down No.2 slipway at Wallsend on 7 June 1945. Completion was cancelled in 1946; she was towed to Portsmouth on 7 July 1946 to be laid up. With her machinery already installed by Wallsend Slipway, she was used for spares, with her boilers going to Dutch carrier ***Karel Doorman*** (ex ***Venerable***) in 1965, and her turbines to the same ship in 1968. She was scrapped at Faslane in the same year. *(Tyne & Wear Archives)*

The other escort carrier built was ***Vindex***, originally ordered from SHWR as YN 1667 in 1941 - as the refrigerated ship ***Port Sydney***. With her 17-knot designed speed, the Admiralty took her over on 29 June 1942. She was launched on 4 May 1943 and renamed ***Vindex***. She left the Tyne on 30 November 1943 to provide air cover for convoys with her 20 aircraft.

Vindex was purchased by Port Line from the Admiralty in 1947 for conversion by SHWR back to her planned refrigerated cargo ship design. Here she arrives back in the Tyne on 12 October 1947. So extensive was the work that a new Yard Number was allocated: 1783.

Vindex moored at buoys for the 150-ton floating crane ***Titan*** to remove redundant equipment, while a smaller crane aft removes the flight deck.

Now unrecognisable as a former aircraft carrier, the 10,480-grt refrigerated ship ***Port Vindex*** steams out into the North Sea on 31 May 1949 for 22 years' further service.

Barfleur (YN 1691) was SHWR's first Battle class destroyer to be built. Ordered in April 1942 she was launched on 1 November 1943, but late delivery of her new Mark 6 director delayed completion, notionally recorded as 14 September 1944. She did not leave the Tyne until 25 January 1945, when this picture was taken. She joined the British Pacific Fleet, where her strong anti-aircraft armament would be useful. She served in the Mediterranean for most of the 1950s. She was scrapped at Dalmuir in 1966.

St Kitts (YN 1695) passing Tynemouth priory and castle, the latter still in the hands of the Army for coast defence until 1956. She was completed on 21 January 1946, the third of five Battles completed by SHWR. Two more were cancelled, although the hull of one, to have been named ***Oudenarde***, was used for postwar tests by the Naval Construction and Research Establishment at Rosyth. ***St Kitts*** served in the Mediterranean in the early 1950s, taking part in the Suez campaign in 1956. She paid off the following year, and after lay-up at Devonport was scrapped at Sunderland in 1962.

Although not completed until after WW2 in November 1945, construction photos of cruiser ***Superb*** (YN 1683) are rare. However, this view taken in June 1948 shows her in essentially her as-completed condition. Compared with earlier cruisers, her 'X' triple 6-inch turret was never fitted, nor were aircraft handling facilities, giving way to improved anti-aircraft weapons, radar, accommodation and boat stowage. She undertook flagship roles to 1957, but was never fully modernised. She was laid up in the Gareloch, and scrapped on the Clyde in 1960.

War in the Pacific required fast oilers. Anglo-Saxon Petroleum (now Shell) had already ordered ***Hyalina*** (YN 1689) early in 1942 with British Thomson Houston turbo-electric machinery for 17 knots. She was taken over as ***HMS Olna*** after launching. Here she has just come out of drydock at Wallsend on 13 April 1945 prior to delivery. Her sister ***Oleander*** (YN 1711) was completed as ***Helicina*** for Shell in 1946. With her replenishment at sea rig, she was employed worldwide until replaced by the 21-knot OL class RFAs in the 1960s.

SHWR completed six cable ships during WW2, two for the Postmaster General (***Ariel*** and ***Iris***) and four for the Admiralty. Two of the latter are seen here at Msida, Malta postwar, on the left ***Bullfinch*** (YN 1660, completed 1940) on the right ***St Margarets*** (YN 1800, 1944). Relatively small ships at 1524 gross tons, they were used mainly for cable repair purposes, but were also available for commercial charter. Both reached forty years of age before being scrapped. Their sisters were ***Bullfrog*** and ***Bullhead***. The cable ship in the background is ***Cable Enterprise*** of 1924.

Lead ship of her class, the destroyer ***Daring*** (YN 1739) glides down the slipway at Wallsend yard on 10 August 1949, after nearly four years on Berth No.5. ***Daring*** and ***Demon*** were ordered in January 1945, but the latter was cancelled in December 1945. In the background is Shaw Savill's cargo liner ***Delphic***.

(Tyne & Wear Archives)

The Daring class destroyers were the first to embody all the wartime lessons learnt, with new twin high angle/low angle 4.5-inch Mark 6 mounts, improved fire control and close range weapons and more advanced machinery spread over separated boiler and engine rooms. ***Daring*** was completed in 1952, as seen here on 12 December. Other ships of the class trialled alternating current electrics and different designs of steam turbine. ***Daring***'s machinery came from Wallsend Slipway, of Pametrada design, whose new research station was next to the Wallsend shipyard. She was scrapped at Blyth in 1971.

Although YN 1721 ***Albion*** had been ordered in July 1943, she was not completed until May 1954. Launched on 5 May 1947, construction was suspended as an economy measure. Seen here under tow to Rosyth for drydocking, her bare hull collided with and sank the collier ***Maystone*** on 18 October 1949 off St Abbs Head. In May 1953, she made 28 knots on preliminary trials on the St Abbs measured mile.

Albion during her fitting out at Wallsend early in 1954. Her 6-barrelled Mk 6 40mm Bofors and its Mark 2M Close Range Blind Fire director can be seen ahead of the island. She had the latest radars – the curved Type 983 heightfinder antenna, and two Type 982M triple paraboloid antennae. She cost £9,836,000, over £0.5M less than her sisters ***Centaur*** and ***Bulwark*** at Harland & Wolff. The Wallsend Slipway contract was £1,870,000, a much smaller proportion of the total than destroyer types. The pound was then worth about 20 times its 2007 value.

Albion leaves the yard in April 1954 aided by four tugs. She is passing the Jarrow coal staith on the south bank, off which two colliers are moored waiting to load. On the north bank is North Eastern Marine's engine works, which became AMEC Offshore. Converted to a Commando carrier in 1962, she was scrapped at Faslane in 1973.

When the Royal Navy needed faster replenishment tankers than the 14-knot Wave class, four 17-knot Tide class vessels were ordered in 1952. SHWR received the order for ***Tidereach*** (YN 1847) seen here on 11 July 1955. Her 15,000-shp steam turbine machinery from Wallsend Slipway gave 18.22 knots on trial. Her primary cargo was 9,000 tons of furnace fuel oil used in the boilers of a predominantly steam powered navy, plus 3,000 tons of aviation fuel and 1,000 tons of diesel oil, more than enough to completely re-supply the biggest aircraft carriers in the fleet - ***Eagle*** and ***Ark Royal***.

Two of the twelve Type 14 anti-submarine frigates were ordered from SHWR. These 'utility' vessels were intended for fast construction in all-welded units in smaller yards than could handle the bigger Type 12s. But with the priority for merchant ship construction in the 1950s, the ships took five years to build. YN 1829 ***Pellew*** is about to be handed over in July 1956. Although with the minimal gun armament of three 40mm, they carried the same sonar and anti-submarine mortars as the Type 12s. She replaced ***Tintagel Castle*** in the 2nd Training Squadron at Portland. By 1970 the Type 14s were completely obsolete and either used for fishery protection purposes or scrapped.

Shipyard workers watch ***Lion*** leave Wallsend on 22 July 1960. Construction had started at Scotts' on the Clyde in 1942 as ***Defence***; she was launched on 2 September 1944, but work was suspended in 1946. She arrived at SHWR in August 1955 to be completed with a new name, new armament and new superstructure. She was scrapped virtually unchanged in 1975 at Inverkeithing. *(Tyne & Wear Archives)*

HMS Lion off the Northumberland coast in July 1960, her hull and machinery very much 1940s in design, but her superstructure, armament and electronics late 1950s. She mounted one new twin 6-inch Mk XXVI gun turret forward and another aft, instead of the designed three triple 6-inch Mk XXIV, plus three twin 3-inch guns, optimised for anti-aircraft performance.

SHWR built only one of the successful Leander class general purpose frigates, YN 1935 ***Galatea***. Here she is seen just completed on 25 April 1964 for the Ministry of Defence (Navy), that ungainly title having superseded the 'Admiralty' on 1 April. Her 30,000-shp steam turbine machinery was the last such set built by Wallsend Slipway for a warship, costing £1.06 million. The hull cost £1.85 million, while the total ship cost including MoD supplied weapons was £4.34 million. Leanders saw service all round the world, with their Wasp helicopter proving a great asset - its hangar and flight deck aft clearly visible. ***Galatea*** was modernised at Devonport in 1974 to carry the Australian Ikara anti-submarine missile forward, in place of her twin 4.5 inch gun. She was sunk as a target in 1988.

The Royal Fleet Auxiliary oiler ***Oleander*** (YN 2004) on trials on 11 October 1965, with 26,500shp steam turbine machinery built by Wallsend Slipway. She was renamed ***Olmeda*** in 1967 to avoid confusion with the frigate ***Leander***. Her sisters ***Olna*** and ***Olynthus*** were also Tyne built, but completed at Hawthorn Leslie before that yard joined the Swan Hunter group in 1968. She was scrapped in India in 1994.

SHWR received an order for three new purpose-built store ships for the Royal Fleet Auxiliary in December 1964. The previous slow 10-knot Fort vessels had been converted from conventional cargo ships and were not suitable for easy stowage and handling of naval stores or keeping up with the fleet. ***Lyness*** (YN 2016), seen here leaving for trials in January 1967, preceded ***Stromness*** (YN 2017) and ***Tarbatness*** (YN 2018). All three were chartered by, then sold to, the US Navy in 1981-3, ***Lyness*** becoming ***USNS Sirius***.

The 18-knot stores ship ***Stromness*** had a large flight deck - although not intended for Harriers despite this demonstration at Chatham in 1977. Her three replenishment at sea rigs handled dry stores, moved around the ship by fork lift trucks and lifts. She was sold to the US Navy in 1983 to become ***Saturn***.

Norfolk was ordered as YN 2019 when the company was still Swan Hunter & Wigham Richardson, but completed by Swan Hunter Shipbuilders Ltd in March 1970, here seen on trials. She was from the second batch of four County class destroyers, whose high freeboard hull was designed to incorporate the anti-aircraft Sea Slug missile magazine stretching internally from beneath the foremast to the twin launcher just visible aft. She became the Chilean ***Prat*** in 1982. Her earlier sister ***London*** was SHWR's YN 1903, completed in 1963.

The Guided missile destroyer ***Bristol*** was designed as one of four Type 82 escorts to defend the planned aircraft carrier CVA-01. Although the carrier was cancelled in 1963, construction of ***Bristol*** continued, partly as a testbed for the Sea Dart missile (aft) and Ikara anti-submarine missile and torpedo forward. Ordered in June 1966 under the SHWR name, she had their highest Yard Number of 2030, before the new company started a new series at No. 1. Although Wallsend Slipway installed her machinery, her steam turbines came from AEI in Manchester and her two Olympus TM1 gas turbines from Bristol Siddeley, later Rolls-Royce. She survives (2007) as an accommodation vessel at Portsmouth.

All five of the Rover class oilers were built for the Royal Fleet Auxiliary by Swan Hunter Shipbuilders (SHS), three at the former Hawthorn Leslie yard at Hebburn (seen in the background) and two at Neptune yard. Here YN 59 ***Gold Rover*** slides into the Tyne on 7 March 1973. It would be a further twelve months before she was completed. She is still (2007) in the active fleet.

The third of the class, ***RFA Blue Rover***, was ordered as Yard Number 8 at the newly formed Swan Hunter Shipbuilders. She is seen here on trials in June 1970, third of the class. Her original two Ruston medium speed diesels geared to a single propeller proved troublesome, so were replaced by Pielstick engines in 1983. She became the Portuguese ***Berrio*** in 1993.

The Chilean destroyers ***Almirante Riveros*** and ***Almirante Williams*** had been completed by Vickers-Armstrongs at Barrow in 1960, their hulls based on the Daring class. Both were modernized in the early 1970s by SHS in collaboration with Plessey. ***Almirante Riveros*** is seen alongside at Wallsend, nearly completed, in April 1975.

Two Type 42 air defence destroyers fitting out at Neptune yard on 14 October 1976. Nearest is ***Newcastle*** launched 18 months previously and ***Glasgow*** launched 6 months earlier. The twin launcher for the medium range area defence Sea Dart missile, 22 of which were carried, can be seen beneath the dockside crane. The large 'double bedstead' aerial of the Type 965 long range radar above the bridge detected targets up to 200 miles away.

Appropriately the first Type 42 destroyer of five completed by Swan Hunter was ***HMS Newcastle*** (YN 61). She ran trials in February and March 1978. Her 4.5inch Mark 8 gun shows to advantage, as do the Sea dart missiles on the twin-arm launcher ahead of the bridge. She was paid off in January 2005 after 27 years service.

SHS' second Type 42 destroyer was ***Glasgow*** (YN 62) here heading out to the North Sea for trials in 1979, flying the Red Ensign as she has yet to be handed over to the RN. Her completion was delayed by a fire on board on 23 September 1976 when fitting out. Leaking oxygen had created a blaze in a lower compartment, possibly ignited by a cigarette, killing eight men.

The Type 42 destroyer ***Cardiff*** riding light at the former Hawthorn Leslie Hebburn yard on 14 October 1976, eight months after arriving as a bare hull from Vickers at Barrow. Although launched at Barrow on 22 February 1974, progress was slow with pressure of other work, so arrangements were made for her to be completed on the Tyne by SHS - a similar arrangement to the cruise ship ***Copenhagen*** in 1973. She was not given a SHS Yard Number, keeping the 1091 from Vickers. She was not completed until Sept 1979, eight years after being ordered. The tanker astern was completed as the Soviet ***Makhachkala***.

Here the Stretched Type 42 destroyer ***York*** (YN 111) has just been launched from Neptune yard on 21 June 1982, surrounded by launch timbers. Lengthening by 50 ft forward improved seakeeping and performance over earlier ships. She would take another three years to complete, at a price of £58M excluding MoD supply items. She and other later Type 42s have soldiered on in the fleet due to delays in building the replacement Type 45 destroyers.

The Iranian Government's replenishment ship ***Kharg*** (YN 98) laid up at Walker yard on 24 May 1981. Her delivery was embargoed due to the Iran-Iraq war. She had been completed in April 1980, but was not finally handed over until October 1984 - minus her OTO-Melara 76mm gun, seen here on the forecastle. Unusually, she had US Westinghouse steam turbine machinery of 26,890shp for a 21-knot speed. The aircraft carrier ***Illustrious*** lies astern.

Illustrious (YN 102) slips into the Tyne on a murky 1 December 1978, launched by Princess Margaret. She was originally designed as an anti-submarine command cruiser, deploying Sea King helicopters. The design was flexible enough to carry Sea Harriers, so she was able to operate as an aircraft carrier.

Illustrious fitting out at SHS Walker yard on 24 May 1981, 13 months before handover, showing modifications to the original anchor pocket seen in the launch view, to improve its stowage. The yard was the former Vickers-Armstrongs Naval Yard, whose 250-ton crane erected in 1930 still stands (2007). SHS were paid £170M to construct her, which excludes MoD supplied equipment like weapons and electronics.

Ark Royal (YN 109) on No.1 berth at Wallsend in July 1980. Here the hull has reached flight deck level amidships, with the island being erected. The narrowness of the hangar is evident, only wide enough for one Sea Harrier, a serious operational handicap. Ordered in 1978 when the company was owned by British Shipbuilders, she is being built on the same berth as ***Illustrious.***

Ark Royal almost ready for launch, nine days before the Queen Mother launched her on 2 June 1981. Her launch weight was 11,170 tonnes, about 55% of her fully loaded displacement. Her twin rudders have been fitted, but not her propellers. The left hand crane is one of the two 180-tonners designed to erect super-tankers. This crane was sold in 2006 to an Indian shipyard.

Ark Royal heads out to the North Sea in October 1984 for one of her many trials. Her builders were paid £210M excluding MoD items, an increase of £40M over ***Illustrious*** reflecting both inflation and enhanced equipment fitted. Both SHS carriers have been extensively used operationally, ***Ark Royal*** herself in Iraq in 2003.

Modern warships are built in units or blocks, which can weigh several hundred tons, including structure and outfit and machinery. Four units for the frigate ***Coventry*** (YN 124) are seen in the Wallsend prefabrication shop in December 1984. Nearest is the stern unit S01, with angled transom, openings for towed array sonar and berthing arrangements visible. In such conditions, it is relatively easy to fit items like pipework compared with when units are already assembled into a hull.

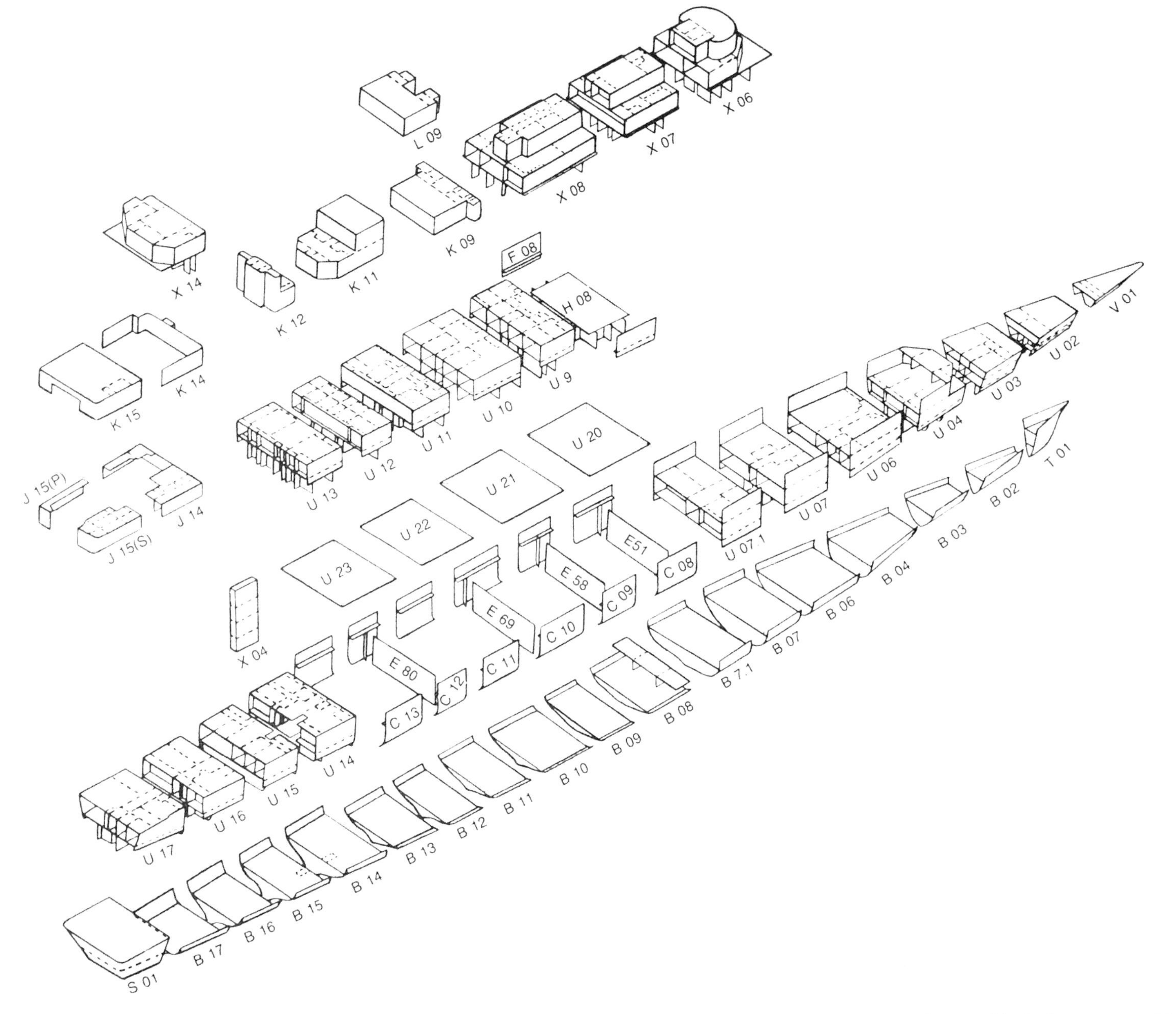

Under 'concurrent engineering', considerable planning has to take place to design, order materials and organise the construction of a warship before any steel is cut. The block breakdown diagram gives a view as to how sixty units made up the complete hull of ***Coventry***. Some shipyards now fabricate considerably larger modules.

The Type 22 frigate ***Sheffield*** (YN 123) on No.8 berth at Neptune yard in 1983. The pre-outfitted machinery spaces are seen looking forward. Nearest the camera is the Aft Auxiliary Machinery Room with two diesel generators in the centre, two auxiliary boilers in front of them with auxiliary machinery modules and distillation plant at each side. The middle compartment is the Aft Engine Room, showing the two Tyne gas turbines and forward the much bigger gearboxes. The further compartment is the Forward Engine Room, although the two Olympus gas turbines are barely visible. Such 'open sky' outfitting before 2 Deck is fitted considerably speeded up installation, protected by the portable Rubb shelters.

The completed ***Sheffield*** on speed trials in August 1987. She had been ordered as a replacement for the Type 42 destroyer ***Sheffield*** lost in the Falklands, although as a Type 22 Batch 2 anti-submarine frigate. Photographed here she has yet to receive her Exocet launchers forward. She became the Chilean ***Almirante Williams*** in 2003. Her sister ship ***Coventry*** went on trials later the same year.

The Type 22 Batch 3 frigate ***Chatham*** (YN 126) passing her birthplace on a visit to the Tyne in October 1990, eleven months after completion. With increasing experience and well planned production, the contract to delivery datewas down to less than five years, having taken 2,500 man-years to build. The Batch 3s had a 4.5-inch gun forward of the Sea Wolf missile launcher for shore bombardment purposes.

Another replacement for a ship of the same name lost in the Falklands was the logistic ship ***Sir Galahad*** (YN 125) on a snowy day early in 1986, six months after keel laying. The machinery spaces are to the left, with vehicle deck and accommodation at sides forward. This berth was later excavated for the floating dock used since 2002 for the assembly of two auxiliary Landing Ships Dock.

Sir Galahad seen leaving the yard in November 1987, the only one of her class. She had been ordered in September 1984. Behind her is the former Hawthorn Leslie Hebburn yard, closed in 1983, while in the distance, ***Sheffield*** and ***Coventry*** can be seen fitting out at Neptune yard. She paid off from the RFA in 2006.

After some hair-raising visits to West Africa by SHS staff, contracts were agreed in 1988 for the overhaul of two Ghanaian fast attack craft. Hauled up on to No.2 berth is ***Dzata*** (nearest) and ***Yogaga***, both built in Germany in the early 1980s. The overhaul work was completed in May 1989. In the background can be seen the WW2 destroyer ***Cavalier***, now preserved at Chatham.

The Type 42 destroyer ***Southampton*** was in collision with the container ship ***Tor Bay*** in the Gulf on 3 September 1988. She was repaired by SHS in their large 850 ft Hebburn drydock, just across the river from the Wallsend shipyard, arriving on the heavy lift ship ***Super Servant 1*** on 24 August 1989. In this aerial view in October 1989, the Sea Dart launcher and 4.5-inch gun have been removed for overhaul. Repairs and modifications took until May 1991. The drydock was originally built for Palmers Hebburn in 1962 when it was a subsidiary of Vickers.

In the spring of 1991, ***Southampton*** built by Vosper-Thornycroft in 1981 shows off her lines in the drydock at Hebburn that now (2007) belongs to A&P Tyne. The yard was modernised for building tankers in the 1970s, with the drydock being used to build several. The Type 42 was the last major RN warship class to be designed in feet units, as revealed by her draft marks forward. She is ready to float out following repair after her collision with ***Tor Bay***.

Fort George (YN 129) was the second Auxiliary Oiler Replenishment (AOR), ordered at SHS on 18 December 1987, with the first unit to the berth in March 1989. Construction has progressed to the upper deck amidships and bulbous bow forward. More modules lie in the foreground awaiting erection. She was completed in March 1993, the same month as her sister ***Fort Victoria*** ordered at Harland & Wolff 20 months before her. In the background can be seen the drydocks of A&P Tyne, formerly the SHWR repair yard.

Two ships on the berth at SHS Wallsend yard on 1 December 1990. On the left, the Antarctic research vessel ***James Clark Ross*** (YN 132) is about to be launched, but ***Fort George*** would not take to the water until 1 March 1991, although the launchways and fore poppet are already in place in this photograph.

SHS first Type 23 frigate ***Marlborough*** (YN 127) on No.2 berth at Wallsend shortly before her launch on 21 January 1989. Clearly visible are her deep bilge keels and non-retractable fin stabilisers fitted to reduce rolling and improve operability of her helicopter and weapon systems, as well as for crew comfort. Drag chains are being placed and the fore poppet inspected, about which the ship will pivot on entering the water. In the background can be seen the twin-funnelled cable ship ***Sir Eric Sharp*** and former destroyer ***Cavalier***.

Marlborough off the Tyne on trials in August 1990. Although externally complete with machinery operational, there was much internal work and testing of systems to be done. The final Type 23 design was extensively altered in the light of Falklands experience, including adding the gun for shore bombardment. The silo behind the gun houses 32 vertical launch Sea Wolf missiles. She was sold to Chile in 2005.

An aerial view of the Swan Hunter Shipbuilders Wallsend yard in February 1991. Alongside fitting out are ***Marlborough*** (right) and ***James Clark Ross*** (left). On the main berth is ***Fort George*** almost ready for launch. In the foreground is the destroyer ***Cavalier*** awaiting preservation alongside the Hebburn yard (now at Chatham) and in drydock at bottom left the cable ship ***John W Mackay***, since scrapped.

One of the Type 23 frigate ***Westminster***'s Rolls Royce Spey SM1A gas turbine modules is shipped on 3 July 1991, seven months after keel-laying. The engine's output was 18774 hp, from a weight of only 25 tonnes.The exhaust uptakes and the power output shaft are on the left. Later Type 23s had the more powerful Spey SM1C turbines. *(Tyne & Wear Archives)*

Westminster (YN 135) on 3 February 1992, the day before her launch, showing her superstructure and funnel structurally complete. Alongside is the lower hull of her sister ***Richmond***. A substantial amount of equipment installation and outfitting has already been done.

(Tyne & Wear Archives)

The Type 23 frigate ***Northumberland*** (YN 136) on No.2 berth early in 1992. Launching ways are fitted and the launching platform for VIPs is in place. The bow swelling is where the dome of the Type 2050 sonar will eventually be fitted below the keel later when in drydock.

Richmond just before the VIPs appear on the platform to launch her into the Tyne on 6 April 1993. The launch weight was about 3,000 tons, with the hull taking only about 40 seconds to enter the water. Also visible are the bilge keels to damp rolling, the active fin stabiliser, and anodes of the hull's anti-corrosion cathodic protection system.

The last surface combatant launched at SHS, ***Richmond*** (YN 137) takes to the water at Wallsend on 6 April 1993, just five weeks before the receivers were called in. The stern has just lifted, with the hull pivoting about its fore poppet, allowing water to drain off the quarterdeck. The drag chains will bring her to a halt shortly before she reaches the opposite bank of the river. She was completed by the receiver in November 1994 under a new MoD contract using many of the previous SHS workforce.

Richmond was the last 'Swan Hunter Shipbuilders' ship to be completed, although actually handed over by the receiver. Although RN manned, she is still under builder's control flying the Red Ensign as she departs from Wallsend on 3 November 1994. The local newspapers asked was this really the end of shipbuilding on the Tyne? However, in 1995, the receivers found a buyer for the yard, which was reconstituted as Swan Hunter (Tyneside) Ltd. Richmond is nearly fully loaded to her 4,200 tonnes displacement.

When the order for two 16,000-tonne Auxiliary Landing Ships, Logistic (later reclassified as Landing Platform Dock, Auxiliary) was received by the 'new' Swan Hunter company in December 2000, they were the first newbuildings since ***Richmond*** left in 1994. The main inclined No.1 berth was excavated to provide a basin into which a floating dock (acquired from Dunkirk) could be positioned. The prefabricated hull ring sections were rolled into the dock on trailers, joined together, then the dock was floated out into the river and moored at the fitting out quay. Here ***Largs Bay*** (YN 141) is being floated out of the partially submerged dock on 18 July 2003, assisted by tugs ***Yarm Cross*** and ***Flying Spindrift***.

The two Bay class vessels were assembled from fifteen large 'ring' cross-sections each about 12m long. The bow unit of ***Lyme Bay*** (YN 142) was fabricated in Holland and here on 18 July 2003 it awaits moving by trailer to the floating dock. Other units were fabricated at A&P Tyne across the river at Hebburn, as well as at the Wallsend yard itself. ***Largs Bay*** is in the background. They are designed to carry troops and vehicles and land them by landing craft or helicopters, being a great advance on the Sir class logistic landing ships they replaced.

The aft end of ***Lyme Bay*** being erected in the floating dock at Wallsend on 19 January 2005. In the centre is the dock well which can be flooded to take landing craft. Her two electrically driven azimuthing thrusters will be fitted beneath the bottom structure. With increasing concern about large time and cost overruns, the MoD cancelled Swan Hunter's contract for her in 2006. The experience of the post 1993 Swan Hunter was in the offshore industry, not in modern shipbuilding.

Lyme Bay had been floated out of the drydock on 3 Sept 2005. The two sisters are seen alongside the Wallsend fitting out quay on 27 October, **Largs Bay** at left. Although externally almost complete, there was still a substantial amount of outfitting and system testing to be completed before handover to the Ministry of Defence. It is unlikely that one, let alone two, newbuildings will ever be seen together again in the Tyne.

Largs Bay left the Tyne for trials on 2 March 2006, before returning to the shipyard for final completion. She is seen leaving on 22 April prior to handover to the MoD and the Royal Fleet Auxiliary on the 25th. Here she is manoeuvred stern first by tug ***Rowangarth*** before swinging to face the sea. The Bays have no funnels, the diesels sited in the wing walls of the dock exhausting through ducts at the end of the flight deck. The vessel was originally due for delivery in early 2004, but she was overtaken by the first of the pair ordered at BAE Systems at Govan, ***Mounts Bay***. The yard in the background is A&P Tyne at Hebburn, with hospital ship ***Africa Mercy*** completing her conversion.

Index